ALASKA BROWN BEAR

A BROWN BEAR HUNT ON THE ALASKA PENINSULA – AN EXTRAORDINARY ADVENTURE

JERRY EDGINGTON

ALASKA BROWN BEAR

A BROWN BEAR HUNT ON THE ALASKA
PENINSULA – AN EXTRAORDINARY
ADVENTURE

JERRY EDGINGTON
ACCIDENTAL ADVENTURE OPPORTUNIST

PUBLICATION
CONSULTANTS
We Believe In The Power Of Authors

PO Box 221974 Anchorage, Alaska 99522-1974
books@publicationconsultants.com— www.publicationconsultants.com

ISBN: 978-1-59433-781-9
eISBN: 978-1-59433-782-6
Library of Congress Catalog Card Number: 2018933907

Remember then: There is only one time that is important—now! It is the most important time because it is the only time when we have any power.
Leo Tolstoy

Kodiak Island

Alaska Peninsula

Aleutian Islands

Bear Scare

We shuffle down the gravel slope on opposite sides of a thicket of alders 50 yards below camp. Circling it is the only practical way to gain a new vantage point. Tate has moved around the west side and I've covered the east side, pausing every couple steps to glass. We both arrive at a clearing just above another alder patch. We're focused on the snow-covered slope across the river, hoping to spot a bear who's chosen this morning to move out of his den. The sun sits just above the mountain to the east and the sky is clear.

"Keep an eye on that snow slope," Tate mumbles. "You'll see nothing, nothing, and nothing, and then all of a sudden he'll be right there and you'll wonder where he came from."

This is the best viewing spot and the best weather we've had all week. The air is still and silent other than my slow breathing and the crunching of gravel under my shifting boots.

Suddenly a panicked shriek pierces the silence.

"BEAR! BEAR! BEAR!"

My binoculars drop to my chest and I follow Tate's stare down the hill. Poking up above the gray alders 30 yards below us is a huge round, brown head with two narrow, beady eyes staring at us.

A shot of adrenaline runs clear though me and I gulp a lungful of air while catching a glint of light from the sun, the exact kind of gulp and glint to produce a sneeze. And in that instant I release the biggest whole-body sneeze of my life. Tate is screaming at the bear, waving his arms and jumping up and down and yelling at me to join him.

The exhilaration of the best sneeze ever leaves me paralyzed for a moment. Then two more sneezes in quick succession. I recover my wits enough to join Tate, who is now yelling, "Don't run, don't run! Just look big and scream!" A second wave of panic hits me when I realize we're both waving empty hands—no guns or pepper spray. What the—?

The sensation of the sneezes and the panic is electrifying and I feel a momentary exhilaration I'll never forget.

The bear remains standing and staring, apparently unimpressed with our shouting, then his head disappears behind the brush.

Our arms drop and we go silent, waiting for what might happen next. "Next" comes immediately as the willowy alders between us and the bear begin shaking— he is moving directly toward us.

"RUN!" screams Tate as he pivots and sprints up the hill. Then ...

Well, let's go back to where this story begins.

The Place

In Southwest Alaska a long crescent-shaped peninsula runs far into the Bering Sea. A place that's about as remote as you can get. Well, at least the most remote I've ever been. And being there feels even farther away than it sounds. It's big, big, open country with broad valleys of rolling tundra and winding streams fringed by snow-capped mountains.

It's a stark and empty landscape, and quiet, so quiet. And when there is sound it's only from the wind and rain. It's untouched, and boringly constant—except for the weather, and this far north and this close to the ocean, it's always changing.

This is home to a few small villages of Eskimo Natives, millions of spawning salmon, and Alaska Peninsula brown bears, huge ones. They're also referred to as Kodiak brown bears or coastal brown bears, or just brown bears. They're all pretty much the same species, the much larger cousins of the inland grizzly.

Getting There

From the copilot's seat of our single-engine six-passenger plane I look down to the Bering Sea. From our low altitude, a narrow white ribbon of water breaking on a gravel shore is visible. The ground is a gray and muted rusty color. It's early May, but there's no sign of spring yet, and there may not be for a while.

Rick, our pilot, shuttles Natives, hunters, and supplies up and down the peninsula a couple times a week, or as weather permits. Since introducing himself and giving instructions to buckle up before taking off, he's been silent. The loud drone of the engine is the only sound. Rick studies the overcast sky in a trance. Dozens of boxes of food and pop, bags of something, and my gear are strapped down in the back behind a cargo net.

A little girl with a pink backpack is buckled into one of the four rear seats. She appears to be about ten years old and is a Native, likely coming to or from a visit with relatives. "Coming in," Rick casually announces into his mike and we begin to lose altitude. A flat dirt runway the size of three football fields comes into view. The plane glides to the ground and we roll to a stop at the distant end of the landing strip near a small rusty pickup truck next to a metal building.

Rick kills the engine and the swooshing sound of the propeller fades. A short round man approaches, wearing a coat with a fur-lined hood that looks built for colder weather. He's a Native, and looks old, with a deeply creased leathery face and a smile absent a couple of teeth.

"Hey Rick," he shouts past me in a halting accent. "Hey Dok," Rick shouts back.

I climb down from my seat and open the back door to let the little girl out. Dok (which must be short for a longer Eskimo name) smiles at the girl and pats her on the top of the head. They obviously know each other.

Dok looks back at me, "You must be here for bear."

"I am," I answer, expecting a follow-up question. There is none and he directs his attention back to the plane.

Rick crawls to the rear of the fuselage and takes down the netting and begins pushing boxes toward the doorway.

"See you brought us some food," says Dok, noticing the boxes

"Yup, and some mail."

Rick hands the boxes down to me which I hand off to Dok to place in the bed of the pickup. The final item is my rifle case. "Don't want to forget this."

"You can wait inside if you want," Dok offers. His accent and style of speech make me feel like I'm in a faraway place and have taken a step back in time. Curiosity draws me to the steel building and I carry my gear to the door. There are no signs on it to reveal its function.

Opening the screen door and stepping inside the function becomes clear. It's a very small grocery store, more like a pantry with dry goods and a cooler for perishables. It couldn't accommodate more than five people at a time. In the corner is an alcove with a rough desk, a dozen mail slots and a communications radio with a free-standing mike—a combination post office and air terminal. Sitting against the wall by the front door is a very small table and two chairs.

Dok drives his pickup loaded with the boxes to the screen door and steps inside. "So you're headed out for bear," he says, picking up the conversation from earlier.

"Yeah, going with Bill."

"I like Bill," says Dok, looking to the southern horizon. "He should be dropping in here soon. Rick's taking another hunter back."

I'm a bit sketchy on the details and getting to this outpost with my gear and gun is all the instruction Bill provided. But he is reliable and Rick is waiting, so I settle in.

Dok enlightens me on how things operate out here. His pickup is the only vehicle in the village, everyone else gets around on four-wheelers in the summer and snowmachines in the winter. And this close to the ocean everything made of metal rusts.

His village is about a half mile from the landing strip and a lumpy narrow dirt road connects the two. Hardware and durable goods arrive by barge twice a year; spring and fall. Everything else comes in by plane.

They eat a lot of fish, a bit of seal meat, and the dry goods. There are no moose or caribou in the area.

"Do you eat bear?" I ask.

Dok wrinkles his face, "Not if I have other meat, like salmon, or moose, or caribou. They're all better than bear, but if I do, I only eat fall bear. You'll see why if you kill one. They fatten up on fish in the summer and fall, which gets them through the winter while they're denned up. So in the spring they're pretty stinky, like rancid fish oil. You trophy hunters are the only ones who take 'em in the spring. That's Fish and Game's fault—the way they set up the hunting seasons. I won't eat spring bear. We get good salmon up the rivers in the summer and fall and smoke 'em or freeze 'em for winter.

"In the fall, if we can get Bill or someone to fly us up to the lakes we'll go try for a moose and caribou. But it's a ways up there, and a lot of fuel, and if we get something then it's an extra trip to get all the meat back. So, we take it if we can get it but the fish is what we mostly live on."

The little girl is sitting at the table reading a book and drinking an orange soda. Dok obviously appreciates my fresh ears, and I like the orientation, so he continues answering my questions as he sorts the new bag of mail.

"So, what do people in your village do when they're not fishing or hunting?"

"Not enough," Dok replies in an annoyed tone, avoiding a direct answer. "We used to do a lot more just to live—find our food and preserve and prepare it. But a lot of that has changed. Too many things are done for us now. Just look around here. We didn't have none of this when I was a kid. No boxes of food or pop and candy, no sleds or four-wheelers. Dogs weren't our pets, they were workers. A lot has changed and it's not all good. But our traditions are good. We still have families and our Elders and we stick together. I like the old days best. But little Nora over there, she has a whole new world out there."

"So, how do the locals feel about the bear hunters that come through here?"

"They don't seem to care much. I'm the one who sees and talks to you guys. I doubt you'll meet anyone else while you're here, just Bill and your guide and Rick and me. And any other hunters you see coming and going. We all like Bill and Rick, mostly 'cause they're our transportation when we need it. There's plenty of bear, so that don't bother 'em. And there's not enough of you to bother the salmon, and you come at the wrong time to fish anyway. So we pretty much don't care about you," he chuckles at his good-natured sarcasm.

Dok pauses to offer Nora another soda, then turns back to me. "You hunted brown bear before?"

"No, this is my first time. So I figured I'd come to the best place in the world for it, right?"

"Yup, you came to the best place. We have good bear. How'd you find Bill?"

I offer some details about meeting Bill and hunting a Dall ram a couple of years ago. This catches Dok's interest and he peppers me with questions about the Dall sheep. Alaska can be many different worlds to the Natives. Some of the Elders like Dok may only ever see One area. This peninsula is Dok's world. The Dall sheep, musk ox, glacier fed rivers, and all the things that happen inland are just stories they hear from others.

I pull a couple of hard caramels from my pack and offer one to Nora, but she shakes her head no, so I toss 'em to Dok.

"So, tell me about your village."

Dok begins reminiscing about his youth. He gets to the part about there being more people in the village back in his day. "Kids got a way out of here these days, so they leave. College and jobs and stuff. And the ones that don't go probably should."

"There's Bill," Dok chuckles without looking up. "I always hear him before I see him."

It takes me a minute to notice the distant buzz and I step to the screen door and look to the south.

The glint of the plane appears low on the horizon and grows until it's overhead and banking west to line up with the landing strip. Twenty feet from the ground the engine cuts out and the plane floats to the dirt, bounces and rolls to a stop 30 yards from the building. The door pops open and Bill jumps down and walks toward us.

"I have your supplies in my truck, Bill," Dok volunteers before greetings are exchanged.

"Good," Bill answers and looks toward me. "See you made it. Any troubles?"

"Nope, things went about like you said."

"Good," Bill comments looking back to his plane. A passenger has climbed out and is unloading his gear.

"I need to give Luke a hand," Bill says heading back to the plane. "He's been out for the past week."

This catches my attention and I follow to meet Luke and hear about his hunt. He's dressed in camo and is tending to the gear at his feet. He looks worn out and his boots are caked with mud. Bill makes an introduction and Luke looks up and extends his hand.

We shake and I pause as I catch myself staring. A long scar crosses much of his face, beginning above his right eye and extending across the bridge of his nose and through his left eye and cheek. His eyelid is scarred over and sunken. I try not to stare, but he appears to be used to curiosity.

"So, how'd you do out there?" I ask.

Luke looks down at his dirt-caked clothes and muddy boots. His appearance tells his story. "Well, all the bear are safe and sound. We covered a lot of ground, but there wasn't much movin', at least nothing I wanted to chase. The one I'm looking for is still in his den."

Coming home empty doesn't seem to bother him, though. Bill would later explain that Luke's scar was from a grizzly attack when he was elk hunting in Montana several years earlier. You can't kill grizzlies in the Lower 48 unless you are being attacked. How does one choose to hunt bear after something like that? Or, maybe one becomes passionate about hunting bear after that? Only Luke knows. Fish and Game pursued and killed the grizzly that attacked him. I'm guessing Luke may have wanted to join them had he not been recovering. I want to hear more about the grizzly attack, but that story will remain with Luke.

Bill begins to load the fuselage with supplies for camp, then my gun case and gear bag. He turns to Luke and they exchange a few words about the coming fall hunt. Luke then heads over to Rick's plane to load his gear.

Bill gives his plane a quick check while Dok reviews some supply orders and scheduling for next week. He doesn't add any fuel so the flight to base camp must not be too long.

I squeeze into the rear seat, buckle in and put on the head phones. Bill slides into the front seat, flips a couple of switches and pumps a lever on the floor like a car jack. He cranks the engine and pivots the plane to head back to the east, then checks the radio for sound and I answer.

He holds the brake, revs the engine, and then releases. Within a hundred yards we are off the ground and banking to the south, gaining a few hundred feet of elevation. "Good trip?" Bill asks over the radio.

"Fine so far," I answer.

"You ready for some tough hunting?" Bill asks. "Don't worry about Luke coming home empty. He was only going to take a really big one. There are some ten-footers out there, but they are late coming out. If you're willing to take an eight- or nine-footer you should fill your tag. This is really good bear country."

"I'm just happy to be here and be hunting," I answer. "Getting is a bonus." A nod from Bill tells me we're on the same page.

I pause here for spoiler alert. I did get a bear. Of course, you knew that when we began or I wouldn't be telling the story, right? But how I got him and what I experienced along the way, that's my real story.

The rolling terrain is a blend of wheat-colored grasses from last fall, gray alder, and rusty orange brush, interspersed with patches of remaining snow in the lowest areas. The ground appears as a lumpy camouflage-patterned rug. In the distance to the southeast, undulating hills give way to small snow-covered mountains. "Looks like it's still pretty cold," I observe the obvious. "At least we won't have the mosquitoes and flies to deal with."

Bill grunts at my tradeoff analysis. "It's not bad, just chilly enough for a slow melt. The bears are a little late coming out and a lot of them den up on the slopes. If there's an upside it's that the snow makes 'em easy to spot.

"Got a warm bag? You won't freeze and you won't starve, so just don't wrestle a bear and you'll be fine. Tate will take care of you."

Base Camp

The empty tundra below feels like a million miles from anywhere. We glide over it in silence until I hear Bill's voice crackle over the headset, "There's home."

Sunlight reflects off the metal roof of a small building adjacent to an open flat field.

We float to the ground, bounce, and roll to a stop in front of the shack. A short, round, disheveled man is standing out front to greet us.

A couple of dome tents and camp chairs sit at the top of a small hill behind the shack.

"It's not much, but it's warm and dry. Oh, and it smells like Mick," says Bill, referring to the round guy. This may also explain the tents on the hill.

I step down from the cockpit and Bill hands me my gear. Tate, my guide for the ram hunt a couple of years ago, appears from one of the tents and comes down. He's a rugged-looking kid with tree-trunk legs and scraggly long blond hair. He's a hiking and packing machine and is built for the wilderness and seems most at home there as well.

"Ready for bear?" Tate asks, offering to help with my gear.

"I am, and it's good to see there are no mountains to climb."

Bill joins in, "Yeah, going after the ram kicked your butt. I'm not sure I would want to put you on that mountain again."

"It did, but I'm thinking this will be different. I'm in a little better shape and I don't see any steep rocky mountains."

The shack is built more for survival than for comfort and it's definitely Mick's domain. A propane stove sits in one corner with a couple of plywood shelves holding canned goods on the wall above. A few cookpots and a frying pan hang from hooks in the ceiling. A half sheet of old plywood sitting on some sawhorses with four folding chairs serves as the table. In one corner is Mick's bunk—a crumpled sleeping bag on top of a well-worn

foam pad. Mick has a pot of stew cooking and announces that food will be ready in a half hour.

"You know where to find us," says Bill as we move outside to some fresh air.

Bill motions to a small shelter next to the shack, "Get with Tate and see what you need. If you're missing anything you'll find it there."

Tate is sorting and packing gear, "Got a sleeping pad?"

"Yup, and a bag and rain gear; the same stuff I had for the ram hunt."

"What you shooting?"

"A 300 Win Mag."

"Good. Ammo?"

"Two boxes, forty rounds"

"How many bears you plan on shooting?" he laughs. "Pack one box. I know you can shoot, but hunting bear is different from ram. We won't be taking any long shots, and once you pull the trigger you need to shoot till you're empty. We can't have a wounded bear. You OK with tarps and no tent? I'd like to stay as light as we can."

"Yup."

"Use this pack. It'll hold more gear and be more comfortable."

He hands me the pack as he leaves and the conversation ends. Tate doesn't waste a lot of words.

I empty my gear bag onto a tarp and start sorting out the stuff I can live without and don't want to pack around for a week. Each item gets more scrutiny than when I packed it a few days ago. I begin a "leave behind" pile; one knife will do, not three; one headlamp and one flashlight, not three; three pairs of socks, not six; one water filter, not two, and so on. "Why did I bring all this extra stuff?" I mumble to myself. It will be here for the trip home. Less is good.

With the essentials now organized in my new pack I head back to the porch of the shack where Bill is looking over his landing strip.

He nods at the two tents on the hill, "You can take the tent on the left. We won't head out till morning so sight your gun and take it easy tonight. Just don't hit my plane," he laughs, "It's a long walk out of here."

I stow my gear in the tent and return to the shack with my rifle and a box of ammo. Tate is waiting and holds up a quart-size coffee can. We walk past the plane and stop at a foot-high ridge of dirt about 20 feet long in the middle of the landing strip. Tate walks another hundred paces and sets the can on a tuft of grass and returns. "It's a hundred yards," he says covering his ears and squinting toward the can.

I chamber a round, drop the crosshairs to the center of the can and squeeze. With the crack of the rifle the can flies 10 feet in the air, drops to the ground and rolls to a stop.

"Looks like you're on. Save the rest for the bear." And he retrieves the can.

Mick announces the stew is ready and we file inside, load our bowls, and move outside to eat.

"So what's the story with your landing strip?" I ask Bill.

"Yeah, nice and flat huh? And I haven't touched it. It's been this way since the old man started hunting here in the '50s. Guess that's why this became the base camp."

"What's with that little ridge in the middle?" I ask, nodding toward the elongated dirt ridge from where I had just shot. "Looks like it's in your way."

"It was here too." Bill answers. "Don't know if someone built it or it just happened to be there, but I'll show you what it's for tomorrow."

We finish up and leave the bowls for Mick.

I climb the hill to my tent, plant myself in a camp chair, and begin to glass the thousands of acres of tundra and hills to the east.

So, these Alaska Peninsula brown bears we're hunting are the biggest on the planet. My only reference point to these are the bears Jay and I saw on the Alagnak River, and they were plenty big, but Bill says these are even bigger.

I'm full of anticipation, not as much about what will happen this week, but how it will play out and how it will feel. Nature unfolding before me, connecting one discovery to the next.

It's stunningly quiet up here on the hill; a stillness I seldom experience except in a place like this. Thoughts and worries of the real world have begun to melt away.

The evening air is cool on my face and the light lingers longer than I can keep my eyes open. The twenty-hour journey to get here catches up to me and I fall asleep on top of my bag on the cot.

A chill wakes me early and I pull on another layer of fleece. I've slept soundly till just now. I step outside to a predawn sky. Steam forms from each breath and quickly vanishes. The eastern sky before me is surreal. A vision of the past, the present, and the future. Overhead is a midnight blue—the night just past. It lightens to the rose-colored glow of early dawn sitting on the horizon—the day yet to live. And a single brilliant star hovers Between the two; a beacon of this moment. Just now and just me and just here. The scene imparts a powerful feeling, an image frozen in my mind.

It's always quiet out here in the wild, but just before dawn seems more so. The first morning after sleeping in the wilderness is an "in the moment" feeling.

The week that lies ahead is free of distractions and people, which is most rare. This week I'm free to discover whatever this country offers, or whatever I'm ready to take in. It becomes my new reality.

The sky slowly lightens and the tundra is revealed.

These unexpected, kind of accidental hunting adventures have their moments of truth. Finding prey, stalking, settling the crosshairs on the kill zone. That instant of squeezing the trigger, when adrenaline is at its peak, hovering between tension and anticipation.

But this star is my moment of truth; this feeling of presence, when I let go and find the feedom of this place, this new cold air and the clear morning sky, at the threshold of the coming moment.

The thought settles on me as people begin to stir around the shack and I wander down.

The Drop-Off

Tate's gear is sitting next to the tire of the plane. There's no weather to contend with and Bill is ready to roll. "Let's get going. I'll take Tate out and drop him and come back for you. You can grab some breakfast. I shouldn't be more than an hour. It's your last chance for some of Mick's cooking for a week or so." He laughs and sends Mick a head nod.

"I'll be here."

Tate loads his gear and squeezes into the rear seat and Bill scrunches into the front.

The engine cranks and the plane rolls to the north edge of the flat and spins a one-eighty. Bill holds the brake and throttles up until the engine is screaming, then he releases. The plane lurches forward like a sprinter coming out of his starting blocks in the direction of the dirt ridge, and within about 80 yards is nearly at takeoff speed. The front tires hit the ridge and catapults the plane 10 feet into the air, like a ski jumper. After a slight dip in elevation they continue to rise. "So, that's what it's for," I chuckle.

They shrink on the horizon and the buzz fades. Mick offers to cook some breakfast, but I decline as politely as I can. I need to have a good stomach for the week ahead and Mick's cooking could pose a risk.

In less than an hour the buzz returns and soon the plane is on the ground and ready for me. We repeat the drill and hit the ridge and take off. Bill glances back at me and grins, "Don't really need it, but it's kind of fun."

We fly close to the ground heading south toward the foothills, framed by snow-covered mountains behind. Several minutes later we cross a wide stream. It's more like a river with long sweeping turns. Gravel bars are exposed in wider sections. Bill locks on to the river's course like a slow-motion laser-guided missile and follows it in a serpentine pattern. My stomach's not great with the extra zigzag motion of a slalom skier. I'm a wimp when it comes to motion sickness. Even the merry-go-round got to me when I was a little kid. Loved the horses, but hated the motion. Finally, we straighten and the engine cuts out just before I lose it. We drift down to a narrow gravel bar. I've watched Bill land on these before, but they've been longer. Clearing the top of the willows we drop the final few feet. The balloon tires bounce on the gravel and we come to a hard stop.

Tate is sitting on his pack in the brush and he comes over to lend a hand as the propeller winds down. We quickly unload my gear and splash across the shallow water to the south bank, where Tate grabs his pack. We keep on the move, leaving Bill on the gravel bar.

We've traveled less than a hundred yards when we hear the plane take off and turn to see it rise out of the riverbed. The whole drop-off has taken less than ten minutes.

We work our way along the riverbank looking for fresh bear sign. "If we're going to pick up any tracks, it's gonna be down here by the water in the sand or mud. There won't be sign out there in the brush," says Tate.

After a half mile of riverbed and no tracks we start angling up a small hill. "Let's get to the top and glass."

By the time we reach the top I'm sucking air, even at sea level. The hill didn't seem long or very steep, but sweat is dripping off my nose and I peel off my top layer of fleece.

Stretching before us are thousands of acres of sweeping valley floor, 10 miles wide and 20 miles long. It's guarded by eight sentinel snow-covered mountains, significant by Alaska Peninsula standards, but nothing sheer like the Chugach range where the Dall sheep live.

This is more country than we could cover in a month, and from where we stand, the mountains to the east are a plane ride away. The cold spring has slowed new green growth and most of the valley remains an earthy color, other than a few small patches that catch the sun.

I couldn't tell you where I was on a map, not even close. Or what rivers run through here, or anything else for that matter. I just know we are somewhere on the Alaska Peninsula and there are big brown bears and little else, other than the millions of salmon throughout the summer and fall. No matter how big I've seen my world before, it just got bigger.

Tate breaks out his binos, "It may still be a little slow, but there are a few of them out there wandering around."

The valley floor is a combination of the muted colors creating an excellent camo pattern. The color contrast of the bears will be slight, and hard to detect. Spotting movement may be the more likely way we'll find them.

After a couple of hours of glassing a breeze picks up and I retrieve my fleece.

"Let's work our way south to those three peaks," Tate suggests, pointing to the mountains about five miles away. "There's a river that runs around the base of the one on the right. We can get a good view of that western snow slope, and down the river."

The rest of the afternoon and evening we move from one hill to the next, glassing along the way until I am worn out. Small streams crisscross the valley and we have good access to water.

"Where you thinking we should camp?" I ask, hinting that I'm worn out from hiking.

"Let's head down by the stream. We'll have water and are more likely to find something soft to sleep on."

We traverse down to a grassy spot on a high river bank across from a gravel bar. Camp setup consists of little more than spreading my two tarps with my sleeping pad and bag in the middle—pretty basic.

"Looks like a sleeping bag sandwich," I laugh. The setup looks inadequate for camping in the Alaska wilderness, but we're traveling light and comfort is an afterthought.

The bottom tarp protects from the moisture coming up from the grass and the top shields from the rain and dew. They'll also lock in some body heat. As sparse as it is, I'm worn out and getting horizontal feels like heaven. Tate levels the butane burner and boils some filtered water.

A couple of cups of hot water added to the freeze-dried dinner pouch and a few minutes later dinner is ready, simple as that. Digging in, I think of how tough it was for Dok and his people to get a good meal like this. After walking all day, hot food by the creek feels like all a guy would ever want.

First Tracks

With a full belly and some remaining light I want to scout the gravel bars for tracks and across from camp is a good long one. "I'm going to head downstream a bit and see if I can pick up any tracks."

"Take your gun and spray," says Tate. "There's enough cover down here that you might get close to something and not see it. Wait, I'll go with you."

Tate is visualizing something I can't, like rounding a bend and running into a bear, or worse—a sow and her cub. I can't forget we're hunting and not on a nature hike, and we chose this place because there's lots of bear. With my gun and spray I cross to the gravel bar, scanning the ground for sign. I won't find any tracks in the rocks, so I continue downstream to where the gravel gives way to sand and mud. Looking down, I see something that stops me in my tracks.

"Hey Tate, check this out."

I'm staring down at the biggest bear track I have ever seen, including when Jay and I floated the Alagnak. And we saw some big ones.

Tate inspects the print and is immediately interested, "These are fresh—like hours, not days. We should've spotted him from the hill." He then chambers a round, like something could be close, maybe just around the next bend, or in the brush beyond the bank. His focus on the track sends a chill up my back. I ready my gun and follow downstream to the next sandbar where we find another set of tracks. These seem bigger and deeper, like this bear has somehow grown. At least in my mind he has.

"The mud is wetter here," Tate mumbles, kneeling by the fresh prints. "You can see how heavy he is in this softer mud. He's a big one."

The print is 2 inches deep and the mud at the edge is crumbled, accentuating the width.

Tate's head is now on a swivel and his wariness is clear. His eyes dart as he follows the direction of the bear's tracks. We pick up one more solid track where the bear steps out of the streambed onto the grass. There's no way for us to track in the grass so we continue downstream hoping to find more.

"There's nothing down here," Tate whispers. "I was hoping he might cross the stream again and we could pick him up, but he must have headed east. Which is probably why we didn't spot him from the hill. All this brush can make 'em disappear real fast. Let's get back up there and take another look. He could be out there a ways and moving, but we might get a peek."

The giant prints in the mud have made a strong impression on me too and I feel a resurgence of energy.

From the crest of the hill we scan the valley floor. "This country hides 'em pretty good," says Tate, concentrating through his binos. "He could be right under our nose and we might not see him. If we do, though, he'll be a shooter. From the size of that print I'm guessing he's a ten-footer." A long pause follows as Tate's words sink in. "A shooter."

We continue studying the valley floor until Tate breaks the silence, "What made you want to hunt browns?"

The unexpected question is followed by another long silence.

"Not sure really. I didn't know why I wanted to hunt Dall sheep either, until after I did. Guess it just caught my imagination. It's never been a goal or a passion or anything like that. When I'd see photos of hunters and mounts, I couldn't really picture how it all came down. So I wanted to find out. Then when Bill called, I thought there's no time like now. I try to not miss out on stuff if I get a decent chance. Like, who knows if it'll ever come around again? It likely won't.

"Now that you mention it, I'm not sure what started me wanting to hunt anything. But it's usually clear after I do. It's the experience of being there, with the animals, in their world that's so far from mine.

"The ram hunt was kind of like that. I may have been in a bit over my head, but I'm glad I grabbed the chance and came out in one piece."

Tate chuckles, "Yeah, you sort of came out in one piece."

"I'm not looking for a huge bear, I mostly just want to be out here where they are. How about you, why do you guide? I mean, you're a great guide and all, but you don't seem like a real people person, no offense or anything . . . I don't feel much like a people person most of the time either."

"Yeah," he answers, "I'd really rather be out here alone—no hunters to guide, and no offense back. But hunters are my ticket. It's either be here with them, or back in town at some job I'd hate. So, it's a good tradeoff. You seem OK, though."

I acknowledge the back-door compliment and the conversation ends and the glassing continues.

After a half hour Tate offers his take on the bear we can't locate, "I'm pretty sure that big guy is gone for good and we're running out of light. He's on the move and looking for food and a girlfriend, so I doubt he'll be coming back this way any time soon. We'll start again in the morning."

As the sun drops behind the hill the night air cools and I tighten up my fleece and add my wool beanie.

Back at camp I slide into my bag with all my clothes, except boots. The pepper spray is next to my pack, which now serves as my pillow, and my gun is within easy reach. The grass under my tarp is soft, but lumpy and I shift around until I am molded into it.

Sleep comes fast, but I wake to the sound of a light rain hitting my tarp. I burrow deeper into my bag to get warm. The rain continues steadily until I fall back to sleep.

Morning

The rain has stopped, but the air outside my tarp feels wet and cold. I poke my head out and in the light of my headlamp discover a dense fog. It's thick, with visibility at about 20 yards in any direction. My light bounces off it in waves and I feel like I'm floating, like the dizzy feeling of flying. It's unnerving to be in bear country with limited visibility, and this is way more than limited—it's just gone. A bear could walk into camp and we'd never even know he's close. Not that we have anything here that might interest him.

Tate calmly boils water for oatmeal and hot chocolate, apparently not too concerned.

This fog feels like a new world, a different place than I've ever been. Like I went to sleep in Alaska and woke up on the moon (or in a cloud hovering above the moon). I feel like the relevance of time has vanished; there's just light or dark or somewhere in between, and it's sunny, cloudy, rainy, or foggy. It's just the earth spinning, and nature being nature.

"This fog happen often?" I ask. "During the night I heard rain, but didn't expect this."

"It doesn't usually get this thick," Tate answers. "Humidity and air temperature pretty much call the shots when it comes to fog. Things change fast this close to the ocean. I've seen fog like this in the morning, and by noon it's sunny, and by late afternoon it's raining. It could even snow on us before we're done. Just have to be ready for anything."

"Does it hang around long?"

"Sometimes. It should burn off in a couple hours, but this thick it may take a little longer."

My plausible weatherman explanation is that this spongy, soaked ground holds a lot of water and when the air warms, the moisture evaporates and fog is the result, maybe.

"So, does lack of visibility bother you? Like a bear being close?"

"I'm not wild about it, but just make plenty of noise and they're less likely to get curious. I try to get above the fog, at least high enough to avoid surprises. I've never run into a bear in the fog and I don't want to, so let's get packed and up the hill and wait for this to lift."

We do, and on top the fog it lighter and we get about 50 yards of visibility. It feels better, but there's no glassing in the fog so we just wait it out.

Adapt or Die

In the dead grass between my feet I notice lace-shaped lichen and a few tiny white flowers. The plant life here has had to adapt to severe weather conditions and short growing seasons, which stirs some thoughts.

"It seems that what survives up here has had to adapt to this country. The blueberries, the bears, and the people too," I comment, still staring at the lichen. "Like, think of it, both ants and mammoths lived a zillion years ago and the ants adapted when the environment changed and they survived. The mammoths didn't. It's the adaptation that allows for survival, right? And beyond survival, it appears they thrive and are pretty happy. Like they get used to life like this."

Tate gives me a funny look, like what brought this up? But he returns his view on the matter. "Things up here struggle to survive. They've adapted by fighting and if they didn't, they wouldn't make it. Stuff up here couldn't live somewhere else, including the bears and the people. They live for the freedom and the space, but also for the fight to get the freedom. Without the struggle it's too cheap, it's less valued. It can't be appreciated for what it is. That's why they live it, the hard life. It's satisfying in ways that an urban life isn't. It's not just the beauty and fresh air, it's the struggle too."

I like Tate's view on the matter. It's much deeper and more clear than mine.

He continues, "For you, being up this far north, out here in nature, is probably about the solitude and adventure, but it's a pretty hard life. You could take it for a couple weeks, maybe even a summer, but it would get too hard at some point. The quiet, the weather, the cold. You'd never last like these people. It's a different kind of struggle for you."

As we talk the visibility grows to about a half mile. We're back in the glassing business and we hike to another vantage point. There's lots of hiking and glassing, but no bear or tracks. This is not discouraging, however. In fact, it's liberating as it gives us the freedom to wander and explore anything that catches our eye. I've quickly become addicted to undisciplined roaming.

Each day, each hike, each hour of glassing continues to peel away the layers of care, even wants. I can't remember a time when I didn't care what happened next, or even what I wanted to happen.

I could really get lost out here, in more ways than "not found." I can get lost in the silence. Hunting is the way I get access to all this, soaking in this wilderness, hiking, glassing, eating, sleeping. Bears are the reason I get to be here, but hunting has lost it's intrigue for now. Of course, that may change if we ever lay our eyes on one.

I understand and accept my vulnerability to this environment. I control nothing other than where I wander or find shelter, what I wear and eat; but choosing those things feels like enough.

Nature, to be commanded, must be obeyed.
Frances Bacon

"Glassing"

Glassing—hunter's lingo for searching for animals in the habitat that might be hiding them, through binoculars, of course. It requires a ton of patience, curiosity, and imagination. The unpredictability of finding something makes it feel like sport, competing with the landscape to discover what it is hiding.

Tens of thousands of acres of open space and the bears' random wanderings through thick country makes for low odds of sightings. It feels a little like we're panning for gold nuggets; not likely, but you never know.

Glassing is how we spend most of our day and I enjoy the challenge, and the rest.

Needles in Haystacks

Hours slowly pass with only a slight degree of anticipation. The landscape is still and seems it may stay that way for a while. Surprisingly, the patience needed for this kind of searching is easy for me, and I'm good at noticing things like differences and changes. And with worn-out legs and back, I don't mind sitting and staring at this intriguing landscape, like a thousand-piece puzzle.

It's like finding a needle in a haystack. It's tedious and time consuming, and if you give up too soon, you get nothing. Same as if you'd never started—animals hidden in the camo of the tundra and you are none the wiser.

These needles, however, are on the move. They appear from nowhere and disappear into nothing, the world that exists just beyond my view. In different light, sun or shade or from particular angles, the subtle color contrasts expose the animals (the needles) standing out in the haystack (the habitat). That's where I gain my advantage—waiting for the changing light.

Good optics and good vision are vital, but patience and an eye to notice differences is much more so. I plot a grid across the valley so I won't overlook an area and begin scanning in horizontal layers beginning close in and moving out; working back and forth until I've reached the farthest distance. It's serene and exhilarating—the anticipation of discovery, knowing it's there, but I just can't yet see it.

Glassing on the Chili (Chilikadrotna River)

I recall and extraordinary glassing experience from a dozen or so years ago.

My son Matt and I were hunting moose on the Chilikadrotna River in the middle of Alaska (another accidental adventure). We had grounded our raft on a gravel bar and hiked up to a high plateau providing us with a great view of a large section of the valley. This was a spot from which we might see something bedded down in the trees, or wandering through the marsh.

We settled in and began to scan the trees across the river. It was late morning and moose were likely already bedded down, which lowered our chances of spotting something, so we were soaking in the sun and drying out from the previous night's rain.

"Check this out," Matt whispered, pointing to our left and just below us. A caribou and its calf came walking along a narrow trail at a brisk pace, their ankles clicking like snapping fingers. They didn't look in our direction and kept on the move.

A half hour later Matt tapped my arm and pointed to a spot about 50 yards to the west. At first, I saw only forms in motion, then noticed the color contrast against the grass. The forms became animals—a brown bear and a large cub loping toward the river. Their thick, dark caramel coats undulated in waves as they glided down the hill. For a moment I couldn't make the connection between what I was seeing and how it might matter.

"Whoah, those are grizzlies," I observed, more calmly than I felt. "My first thought with that waving hair was that it might be a musk ox or something."

After a pause Matt laughed, "You've seen musk ox out here?"

"No, but I haven't seen bears either."

"What do you think they're running from?" he asked.

"Well, I have a guess and it's probably up in those trees. I don't think they'd run without a reason. I've heard that male grizzlies don't like cubs and will kill 'em. So I'd guess mothers with cubs keep away from them. "

"So, if they're running from another bear, and he's up in those trees, maybe we should move too," suggested Matt.

It was a good and timely suggestion and we gathered our gear and headed upriver. After about 100 yards we encountered a thick swath of aspen trees and alder brush. Matt decided to work around them on the upper edge to see if he could roust a bull moose out of it's bed and check out some other vantage points. We agreed to meet a mile upriver. I headed straight through the trees along a network of narrow game trails. The brush was thick and it felt like a different world in there.

Eventually I broke out of the trees and found a good spot on a ridge to glass. On the far bank was a thick stand of aspen, with dark green spruce trees scattered among them. The leaves had turned yellow and about half had fallen. It looked like a good spot for moose to bed down. I was was guessing at this as I'd only ever seen elk bed down during the day, but moose might be similar.

I reached for my binos, but they were not on my shoulder where they usually were. Matt must have them, I thought, but why would he? I settled in and began glassing through the scope on my rifle while I waited for him.

A half hour passed and no Matt. I stood and walked up and down the ridge to make myself visible in case he might be looking for me farther upstream. From this angle I saw that the swath of trees extended to the base of the mountain. Matt would have had to walk through them as I had, but he'd been gone a while.

The possibility of a bear being up there made me a bit uneasy. I scanned the tree line again and saw a very small form moving. Then the color of Matt's clothes came into view.

I whistled and he headed in my direction at a steady trot.

Arriving out of breath he huffed, "There's something up there that just scared the crap out of me."

"Like what?"

"Couldn't tell, I just heard branches breaking, and we had been talking about bears so I didn't hang around and see what it was."

"I thought you might have gotten turned around, but running into a bear would have been worse. Think it could have been a moose?"

"Maybe, but I didn't stick around to find out. Anyway, this looks like a good spot."

"Yup, all I need is my binos. You got 'em?"

"No. You had 'em where we saw those bears. Put 'em in your pack?"

"No. They were right here on my shoulder when we left."

I checked the outside pockets on my pack, just in case. Now I was getting anxious. Other than my gun, my binos were my most critical piece of equipment and they'd vanished. Finding moose or anything else would be next to impossible without them.

I either left them at our last spot or lost them between here and there, so I retraced my steps in my mind, looking for a hint.

"I'll head back to see if I left them where we were glassing or maybe dropped them along the way."

"OK. I'll stick here and glass. Watch for bear."

I tried to retrace my steps, but knew that finding my binos would be even harder than spotting a moose, much harder. They were small and black and could be anywhere. This had become a much smaller needle in a much larger haystack. There was so much ground to cover, and my chances of finding them diminished with every step. Arriving back at our previous spot I scoured the ground, but found nothing.

I try not to bother God with things I can, or should, take care of myself, but finding these was a pretty big deal—if we were going to have any chance for success I needed them. And I do believe in asking for help when needed. So I sent up a pretty simple and quick request and headed back to meet up with Matt.

You're probably not surprised at what happened next, or why would I be telling the story, but the way it happened was pretty awesome. I headed back into the trees along a trail I thought I had taken originally, but there were too many to be sure.

I moved slowly, scanning the undergrowth along the path. It was thick enough that if they had dropped in there I could be standing right over them and not notice. This felt like a waste of time. I was not even sure if this was the trail I had taken the first time I came through. I kept at it for a few more minutes and then decided to give it up and head back and make the most of glassing through my rifle scope.

I followed the trail for another twenty steps, and Bam! Right there in front of my eyes, hanging from their strap on an alder branch at shoulder height were my binoculars. Right out in the open, like there was a flashing beacon on them. There was no way I could miss seeing them. They must have caught on that branch and pulled off my shoulder when I was walking through and got hung up right where they came off, or another way. Regardless, I whispered a, "Thanks a lot. I know that must have been one of your angels helping me out, and I appreciate your making them impossible to miss." I was relieved and grateful for the little miracle and hustled back and relayed my story to Matt. He chuckled and shook his head and we got on with the task of finding moose.

I glassed in a horizontal pattern over and over, but saw only trees and brush. Then I noticed a little spec of dark tan about a half mile away. It was oblong and about a tenth the size of a jellybean, a caramel one. I assumed it was a rock as it was dead still, but made a mental note and continued scanning.

"Let's keep an eye on that spot," I said. "It looks a little out of place."

I glassed other areas, but saw nothing and kept coming back to the caramel colored spot.

From downstream I heard the faint buzz of a plane. A few seconds later we saw it flying upriver a few hundred feet above the water. Its elevation was slightly lower than our position on the hill and there were numbers and letters across the top of the wing. It passed and veered to the right, making a big circle above us before sinking to the ground.

"Wonder where he's gonna put that down." Matt muttered.

The question didn't register with me as I continued to glass across the river. "Whoah, check out that spot we were watching." The spot of tan moved and became the antlers of a bull moose with a black body. Matt looked, and as he did a second bull stood. "I could have watched that spot all day and not found them if they hadn't moved."

The big balloon tires of the plane touched down with a bounce and it stopped fast. The moose were now moving up the hill and within seconds were out of sight. The plane door swung open and a friendly-looking guy with a green shirt jumped down from his seat.

"Looks like we've got Ricky Ranger," Matt muttered under his breath.

"Howdy, guys. Looks like you're out here for moose. My name's Stan, with Fish and Game."

"Yup. Those two," Matt answered, making a joke of Stan's plane rousting the two out of their bed.

"Yeah, I saw those. Doubt they would have hung around for you to cross the river and get any angle. It's pretty thick over there."

I agreed with a nod, knowing we would have had to line the raft up the river a half mile (impossible), cross and then put on a world-class sneak.

"I just need to check your license and tags real quick."

We made small talk with Stan as we found and handed them over. "I'm surprised you could land up here," I commented.

"There aren't many places I can't put her down along the river if I need to," Stan answered confidently. He handed our licenses back. "I'll leave you guys to it. There are some big moose downriver. You won't be disappointed."

With that Stan returned to the plane and was airborne within a couple of minutes.

"That's crazy," said Matt.

"You mean Stan landing on this?"

"No, that the spot we were watching ended up being two moose."

Like finding a needle in a haystack.

Raw and Real

The air has remained wet and cold the past few days. Since the fog first set in it's been a bit rough. There's been no more fog, but we've had rain off and on, and some wind.

Tufts of tundra grass shutter in the stiff breeze from the west and dense clouds are ready to release more rain. It's midmorning and the night chill still hasn't abated, but it's mostly coming from the wind. A few times during the night I woke to the sound of the rain popping against my tarp. The tarp's been great, better than I'd imagined. It's kept me dry and my sleeping bag cocoon has kept me warm enough. And in the morning all I need to do is stuff my bag in its gallon-size sack, roll up the tarp like a newspaper, and tie it to my pack.

This moment feels raw and sketchy and isolated, but invigorating. There's a lot of exposure out here and a feeling of vulnerability that must be embraced, or at least accepted. It doesn't feel like helplessness, just a respect for nature's realities. There's nothing quite like it, really nothing.

Security is mostly a superstition. It does not exist in nature, nor do the children of men as a whole experience it. Avoiding danger is no safer in the long run than outright exposure. Life is either a daring adventure, or nothing.

Helen Keller

The days are passing quickly and I'd like to slow them down a little. Today feels like it may be different, in a goods way. I don't know why I think that; it's just a feeling, and I'm going with it.

It continues to rain off and on. Cold and discomfort are a just part of being out here and I don't mind and wouldn't change it if I could. It's a choice to be either content or miserable in this weather. I choose content, and with my fleece and rain gear the weather doesn't bother me much.

We continue to hike and glass, hike and glass, moving toward the snow-covered mountain to the south. It's been pretty silent all morning. There's little need for conversation when we're hiking. The rain starts slapping my hood and the breeze turns to wind. We're shut down for any long-range glassing until it stops and Tate suggests we find a spot on a side hill under some alder brush to hunker down and get a break from the wind.

Through an opaque veil of rain at a wind-directed angle, I continue to glass, adjusting the focus rings, but there's nothing to see beyond 50 feet so I give it up. My fingers poking through the openings in my fingerless wool gloves have turned pruney.

The rain popping on my hood sounds like the loud and fast beat of music. Right now it's ACDC, "Dirty Deeds, Done Dirt Cheap."

The best thing one can do when it's raining is to let it rain.

Henry Wadsworth Longfellow

As the time passes I drift in and out of trances and my mind is empty. The rain finally slows to a drizzle and the low clouds begin to lift, fluff, and float to the east in a breeze.

My body heat is gone and the chill of sweat-soaked clothes against my skin returns. I need to generate some warmth and we grab our packs and continue our trek toward the south.

After hours of steady trudging we crest a hill at the west edge of the valley and find a flat spot to take a break. The wind has moved the clouds off to the east and the weather has taken a notable turn. The sun emerges through high clouds and the breeze dies. Between the sunshine and the hiking, I've regained my body heat and shed my pack, boots, and top layer of fleece, and settle into a mound of soft grass ready to glass. The sunshine is welcome, and more valued after its absence. This is the first we've seen of it in a few days. I lie back on my pack to soak it in and melt into a sleep, a deep sleep. It's one of those unconscious states where time completely disappears.

I could have been out for five minutes or fifty minutes, but it felt like a different world in there. A chill stirs me to consciousness and I pull on my fleece. I get my bearings and notice Tate staring off toward the mountain, deep in thought.

"You think much about this world," I ask, "like how it all works—bears hibernating, salmon spawning, that kind of stuff?"

"Hmmm, not really. I notice it, but can't say I really think about it much. I'm out here a lot. I see nature happening and I like it. It's the only place I really want to be. But I don't think that much about how it all works. You think about that stuff?"

"Yeah, when I'm out here and in it I do. I don't get to these kinds of places often and it's usually a hunt that takes me this far away and this immersed. Sometimes I think of not just how it works, but also why."

Tate continues to glass and chuckles, "That's deep. You sound like you might be a spiritual guy. Like you believe in a creator and all that."

"Yeah, I guess I am. The way I see it a Creator made all this, and made me too, so yeah, guess that gives me a spiritual view of things. How 'bout you?"

"Nope," comes the answer, quicker than I expected. "Well, not in the traditional sense. Seeing all this and being in it is the only world I value and the only one I want, but I can't believe a Creator made it."

"So what's your take on how all of this came to be?" I continue.

"It just did, I don't believe in a Creator, that someone made all this. I guess just like you can't believe someone didn't."

The complexity of all that's here gives some credence to Tate's viewpoint. It is pretty incomprehensible at almost all levels.

"Yeah, guess we're different that way." I respond.

The conversation dies and we return to soaking in the sun in our different worlds.

I don't understand the hows of most everything I see—guess that's the definition of a miracle to me, beyond understanding. Like gravity, or energy, or sound, or hearing, or understanding words. Like how a radio even works? I know the explanation; a signal goes up to a satellite (and who thought of putting one of those up there, and how does it stay in orbit anyway?) and beams it back here and is transformed into a sound that my brain can interpret and cognitively translate into some meaning which then elicits a feeling, or a need, or an action.

And then how jumbo jets (or anything for that matter) flies. Engines, electricity, nuclear energy, and I can go on and on. These are explained in books, the miracles we see and experience every day. I know some inspired humans figured it out and made it work. But there are few who really understand it, the physics of the natural world that allow all this to happen.

Then take something infinitely more complex— nature. Like the instinct of a salmon to spawn, to fight their way upstream to where they were hatched, then lay their eggs and die. That's nature's miracle on a level that is unfathomable to me. It just happens that way? Or, it's instinct. What the heck is instinct anyway? I don't get it. For me, it can only be the design of all things according to the laws of nature.

Whoah! I don't find myself in this mental place often and it leaves my head spinning. It also compels me to humbly acknowledge a greater power, a Creator, and that I'm as much a miracle as everything else out there. In fact, my own Being is the biggest miracle I can possibly contemplate, being "Me," living my life.

As sometimes happens, I'm overwhelmed by the complexity of what I do not understand. Then comes something quite opposite, a feeling (not a cognitive recognition) of the simplicity of the design, the natural laws. I don't need to figure it all out to know it's there. I just need to experience it, appreciate it, and feel it.

A wave of peace melts into me. These thoughts are very rare—clarity, connection, and understanding.

Being here is transformative—Tate's view or mine, our personal lens, our perspective, our agency. What a world we have, right here.

Yeah, this bear hunting is a pretty mind-expanding experience, isn't it? I chuckle at the irony that I'm seeing all these connections in nature, these epiphanies, and chasing a bear is how I got here. Clearly, finding a bear has become an afterthought and I'm not sure I'd know what to do if I saw one.

Well, this is a hunting story and I'll get back to that in just a minute, but all of this thinking recalls another remarkable experience. It's a quick little rabbit trail, and a really good one, so follow it with me for a minute.

Doc. . . . the Sun . . . and Connections

My freshman year of college I had a class, Anatomy and Physiology. It was where I really started to learn about how the world worked, how things fit together. My professor—we referred to him as Doc—was very down to earth and plain spoken, and crazy smart.

His first lecture was a class overview and began with intelligence, all knowing, all understanding and so on. He asked what we hoped to learn in class. For most of us it was just a step along a path to graduate; a credit on our transcript.

Then Doc said, "You'll learn things about this world you live in and about yourself that will blow your mind." What professor talks like that? He had my attention.

"You'll not just gain information, you'll gain understanding. You'll see the miracles and the connections of this world, how things fit together and how they work. And how we can understand it through science and reason." He explained things in a way that made sense, that nothing exists in isolation, that one fact begets the next. That there is not only connection, but dependence of everything on everything else.

So, one day Doc's talking about energy and starts connecting dots for us.

"Energy is everything," he said, "You listening to me talk right now is using forms of energy. I'm generating sound waves and your ears are picking them up and your brain is interpreting them, and for some of you who are paying attention it's making some sense. There's more to it, but you get the idea.

"And there's a feeling you get when you understand what you're learning, when you know it's right; it resonates. Those aha moments. That's what learning truth feels like. You'll see as we go on.

"Energy starts with the sun. It comes to earth through light, 'light energy.' That energy is transformed through miraculous processes so we can use it here on earth. So, what are some ways we capture and use that energy?

"OK, let's work backwards for a minute, kind of retrace our steps from the energy of motion, like you moving your pencil to put notes on the page. Don't worry just yet about the next step of reading and understanding them.

"So, your muscles move as your brain instructs them to. It sends messages through nerves to your muscles and you move your pencil. Then, with your eyes you see what you wrote and your brain takes that information back and so on, you see." There was a twinkle in Doc's eye as he imparted the most basic, but most magical miracles of human existence.

The complexity of the human organism is amazing to me, the miracles of how anything happens.

He continued, "Movement—your muscles contracting requires energy, which is formed within the mitochondria in your cells." We then learned about something called ATP changing to ADP and releasing a phosphate, something which transforms energy in our muscles. Yeah, I was really lost at this point, but I had that feeling he was talking about earlier, that kind of undeniable realization that all of this really did happen through a process that fit together and made sense (or at least would at some point).

The sun gets energy to me by first transferring it to plants that I can eat. Or I eat the animal that eats the plants (just another step in the process). It then gets into my cells through a bunch of biological transformations and gives me the ability to move and think, and come out here and hunt.

The salmon that will come up these streams in a few months have been feeding in the ocean on creatures that got their energy from the sun's source as well. It gets transferred to the fish and from the fish to anything that eats it (like a bear), and if nothing does, it lays its eggs and begets the next generation and dies and what's left of its energy becomes fertilizer for the plants that grow along the stream or the little creatures that eat it. It just keeps going, transforming from one form to another.

Doc was getting close to wrapping up and slowed it down a bit to let us catch up. "This is just the beginning, but it's exciting, isn't it? I know by the look in your eyes that some of you have got that feeling I mentioned. You'll leave here with a profound sense of awe and get just a little peek into how it all works.

"Everything you see and do in your short time on this earth is a miracle. You can learn it and understand it, but more than anything else, you can feel it. So, watch it, study it, appreciate it, and feel it. Now get out of here and take a walk in that sunshine, and soak in some of that energy. Go on, git."

That's when I began to notice the connection of one thing to another and it's kind of been that way ever since. And I see it here, sitting on this hill overlooking the expanse of the valley, and feeling it all.

Back to the Tundra
and the Bears

The shadow of a single high cloud passes overhead and the soaking warmth vanishes for a moment. I zip my fleece and pull my hat tight.

After a long silence Tate asks, "So, how do you figure all this came to be?"

"How? I have no idea of how or even why," I answer. "It's way beyond me, but I think this giant puzzle all fits together, like there's a design to it. But for now I'm kind of like you, I just appreciate it, I feel it."

Tate nods and we continue to glass in silence.

The Knoll

The afternoon slips by with no bear sightings and we consider our next move. On the valley floor about a mile from our ridge is a beehive-shaped knob. It sits directly across from the mountain we've been moving toward for the past five days. It appears to be a good lookout point and becomes our next destination.

"Take one more, good look at that west slope," says Tate, nodding toward the facing mountain. I scan it twice and see nothing and start gathering my gear when I hear Tate. "Hold on, may have something here." He points me to the south, low on the mountain about 2 miles out.

"What do ya think?"

Tate watches for another minute in silence. "Well, it's gone now. Disappeared in all that brush. Couldn't tell it's size and over there is pretty nasty country so I say we move on to the knoll."

I'm quick to agree and with my most recent epiphanies am not too motivated to chase anything, at least without more solid information.

We cross a couple of streams, or the same winding stream twice, before reaching the foot of the knoll. After a long drink and filling our water bottles we head up the long slope, winding around clumps of low brush and alder thickets. The top is pretty flat, with lichen-covered rocks and a few tufts of dead grass. A shallow, wide river winds around the mountain we've been watching. It's a spectacular setting and gives us a perfect vantage point from which to see the entire valley and the snowy slope of the mountain

Just beyond the river at the base of the mountain is a sheer rock wall that appears to have been sliced straight

though by a giant ax. The 50-foot-high rock exposure is a backdrop to an elevated flat meadow, half the size of a football field. It resembles an outdoor amphitheater and will become the stage for an incredible show (more on that in a minute).

It will be difficult for anything to wander past us undetected—a big change from our fog-covered camp by the stream. This will be our camp for the night. My legs are again beat and I welcome the chance to settle into a tuft of grass and watch the landscape.

The Bear Pair

The late afternoon sun sits underneath a cloud bank casting a reflective glow on the snow-covered slope. If bears were coming out, they'd be easy to spot.

It's so quiet out here. The sentinel mountain peaks across the valley to the east are about 10 miles away. From that distance something the size of a bear would not be visible, not even through the spotting scope. I glass in horizontal lines across my imaginary grid, beginning from the base of the knoll moving toward the east. On my third pass, about halfway across the valley floor I pick up a tiny dark spec. Used to seeing only landscape, I dismiss it as a rock and move on. On my next pass the spec has divided into two pinhead-size spots against a light background. It's so far away that I locate a reference point to keep track of them; a snow field on the mountain behind.

The slight jiggle of my binos at this distance makes it tough to know if there are really two and if they are moving. "Come on, come on, be something more than a couple rocks," I whisper in my mind, continuing to focus on the landmark until it slides slightly to the right. Wait, landmarks can't move so that means my specs are moving. They now have my full attention.

"Hey Tate," I whisper. "I may have something at one o'clock. Two specs about five miles out, just under the longest bright patch of snow at the base of the mountain."

Tate quickly finds the spots. "Yeah, you might. Too far to know what it might be though, so keep an eye on it and see if it moves."

"It already has a little, but that's all I can tell."

At this, Tate breaks out the spotting scope and steadies it on the short tripod and leans in, adjusting the focus knobs. Then a long pause, "Yup, we've got bear. Take a look."

I do, but see only slightly larger specs. "How can you tell?" I ask.

"Mostly because that's the only thing that would be out here and moving. And it's definitely something. Pretty sure it's bear."

Over the next hour the specs grow to ant size, moving in and out of view among the willow patches. Even through the 45-power spotting scope they remain very small, but grow slightly larger each time they appear.

Another hour passes in silence and the bears close the distance to a mile, following the river at the base of the mountain and in no hurry.

"It looks like a boar and a sow," Tate whispers. "I can't tell for sure but the second one is a lot bigger than the leader. And that would make sense this time of year."

"How do you figure?" I ask.

"Well, it's a little hard to tell their size, but if they're adults, the boar would be following the sow because he's interested in mating. And if she doesn't have a cub (and she doesn't) she's interested too. Likely coming into season. On the other hand, if it wasn't a pair of adults it would be a sow and her cub, but she would be leading and the cub following and even a three-year-old cub wouldn't be as big as his mom yet. So that's how I figure that."

I grunt at Tate's logic and am now convinced we are looking at two mature bears.

At a thousand yards they both emerge from the brush on the far side of the river, still in single file.

They make their way up to the clearing at the base of the rock wall across from us, the natural amphitheater. The meadow is a mix of emerging green grass and the dried wheat-colored grass. They begin feeding on the green patches like horses grazing in a field. I've never seen anything like this before, but then I've never seen bears in the wild, in the spring. I heard on some National Geographic program that they do this. Maybe it's to clear out their digestive systems, which would make sense to me. With a metabolism that has been pretty much shut down all winter, maybe they could use some high-fiber grass to get their system cranked up again, or maybe they just like it.

"What do you think Tate?"

"Let's just watch 'em awhile and see if they move toward us, but with the river in between us that's unlikely. That boar is big, definitely a shooter, but there's no cover for us to get close enough without being seen and I don't want a long shot. The air is not in our favor, and it's getting pretty late. If we were able to get him on the ground we'd be out of light before we could get him skinned out, and skinning a bear in the dark with other bears around is risky."

That's a lot of "ands," so I'm content to just keep watching.

Tate's observation that the two are a couple and traveling together for a reason looks right. They are clearly interested in each other and roll around playfully in the meadow. There's lots of sniffing and mating going on too, like every few minutes.

"I thought these guys mate in the fall and have their babies in their dens in the winter."

"Part of that is right," Tate answers, sounding like a wildlife biologist. "The part about having their cubs in their den. But they mate in the spring, and pretty often as you can see. They'll hang out together for a week or so, until she has some fertilized eggs. Then her hormones will change and she'll lose interest and ditch him, or he'll ditch her; not sure who does the ditching but they lose interest and become solitary again. I seldom see more than one bear at a time other than a mother and cubs, or a pair of older cubs starting out on their own. They lead pretty solitary lives.

"When they part ways she won't be interested in males until after her next cubs are raised and gone, which is usually around three years. This is the crazy part though—one of those miracles of nature you were talking about. The fertilized eggs won't start to grow until fall. Guess that's when she's officially pregnant. They just sit there all summer waiting for the right conditions."

I'm taken back by Tate's answer, partly because of the miracle of the bear's reproduction and partly because I haven't heard Tate say that much at one time.

"So, I'm guessing the right conditions might be if she's fattened up enough to last the winter in her den, have her cubs and feed them until they come out in the spring?"

"Guess so," Tate answers, continuing to elaborate.

"She obviously wouldn't be mating if she still had her cubs with her, and they usually hang around for three years. In fact, she'd be staying as far away from males as possible because they'd kill her cubs. So, it's either her first time coming into season or she ditched her cubs last fall and is ready to reload."

"So, what's with the boars killing the cubs?"

"Because when the sow's not taking care of her cubs, she'll come back into season and be ready to mate again. Maybe it's also because the survival of the boar's gene pool only happens with his own cub's survival. Knocking out the competition. Either reason, or both—it's the way the boars roll, like survival of the fittest."

"Where'd you learn so much about bears? I thought you just guided hunts, but you sound like a biologist or something."

"Just picked it up here and there from guiding hunters, the smart ones anyway. Most of this stuff I learned from a dentist I guided a couple years ago. He knew a lot about bears and was a talker, and we had lots of glassing time.

"Most hunters don't know that much about bears. They just want their bear and bigger is better. The more I've learned about 'em though, and the more I watch 'em, the more I respect 'em and like 'em. They are pretty amazing creatures."

"So, is it hard to hunt 'em when you know this much about 'em?"

"Naw, actually the more you know about them, like their nature and behavior and the dynamics of their world, the easier it is. The anti-hunters think you should just leave 'em all alone. But they don't know enough about 'em. Like, take this female, after the boar's done his part she'll leave him and wander and just eat as much as she can for the next six months or so. Then the fertilized eggs will get to where they're supposed to be to start growing. She'll be good and fat and den up. A few months later she'll have two or three little one-pound cubs. Then she'll nurse 'em until spring. They'll put on ten or fifteen pounds and come out of their den and she'll keep feeding 'em and teaching 'em, and protecting 'em for two or three years and then turn 'em loose. Then she'll find another boar and do it all over."

As Tate goes on I think about those connections Doc always talked about, miracles now evident in the world of bears.

Tate continues with his philosophy on hunting, "Since the biggest threat to the cubs is running into a big boar, shooting a few mature males each season doesn't bother me. Taking a boar out of the food chain gives a few dozen cubs the opportunity to survive. Gives the next generation a better chance.

"The cubs have enough adversity as it is, and the boars make it worse. Bill has permits for a handful of bears each year in this area. And there are a few hundred, so to my thinking, taking a few is actually pretty good ecology. Good for the bear population in general. And males don't usually kill other males. They'll fight some for the breeding rights, but seldom kill each other. But a cub around a boar is pretty ugly."

This narrative from Tate is fascinating. I had no idea about all this behavior and survival. Out here in nature these miracles are pretty clear, and our pace is slow enough for me to notice them (another reason the weather never bothers me).

The past two hours have been energizing. The camouflage pattern of the valley absorbs the bears and this hilltop location gives us an advantage so I'm content to stay right here until we find something to stalk.

The bear couple have occupied our full attention for the past hour. Then Tate's words, "He's a shooter" hits me. If they did start wandering in our direction and got to within range, would I shoot? It's an odd thought since I am bear hunting and this male looks really big, and with Tate's recent tutelage, it would be the best and right thing to do. But I'd almost hate to break up this happy couple, at least tonight. Though they don't mate for life, I'd like to give them enough time to ensure that this mother bear will be walking around with a couple of cute cubs in the spring. It looks like they've settled into this spot for a while and I won't have to make that decision.

Competition

"Whoah, check this out," whispers Tate. A hundred yards upstream a single large bear emerges from the brush. With his keen sense of smell it's a good bet he has noticed the sow and is now headed in her direction.

The newcomer rounds the bend in the river and comes into full view of the couple. The sow quickly shuffles up by the rock wall and plunks her butt down on the grass, like she knows what will happen next and is ready for the show. Her mate moves down the hill and meets the intruder with a loud warning roar that we hear distinctly from 600 yards. The bellow bounces off the rock wall and echoes across the valley. Through my binos the two appear about equal in size, both very large.

"We've got a couple of nine- or ten-footers," Tate whispers, like they might hear us as easily as we hear them. The two begin sizing each other up, like boxers in the first round of a prize fight. They arch their backs in an exaggerated intimidating posture and begin bawling at each other like dueling foghorns.

The first bear is on higher ground and rises to his hind legs, arches his hump and presses his head forward. The intruder mirrors his movement.

"This is freakin' amazing!" Tate chuckles.

It first appears to be a battle of bellows, an attempt to intimidate the other into leaving without an actual battle. Then suddenly they engage. Claws flying and fangs slashing in a giant spinning fur ball. Loud bawling snarls bounce off the rock wall for ten long seconds. Then as quickly as they flew together they part and resume their stare-down. Neither seems much damaged by the encounter.

After a half minute they're back at it. A spasm of fur bouncing back and forth like an electric arc, then another sudden break. The boyfriend remains on the uphill side of the fight and appears to be more motivated.

Another brief pause and the third round begins, but lasts only a few seconds and intruder is pushed backwards down the hill. He backs away then turns and runs, glancing back twice while splashing across the shallow water.

The winner stands guard on his haunches for a long moment before returning to his mate, who has watched the entire show nonchalantly. The fight has not dampened their mood, in fact, it seems to have intensified it, and they resume their play and coupling in the fading light.

I'm awestruck by the spectacle we have just witnessed. "So, how often do you see something like that, Tate?"

"Once, counting this time," he laughs. "I've never seen anything like that. I've watched a lot of bears, mostly during hunting season, but I've never seen anything like that—that intense. And that sound echoing off the rock made it feel really close."

The bear that was run off has disappeared into the camo field of brush on our side of the river, a fact I note with some uneasiness.

"What are the chances the loser might be checking us out later?" I ask.

"Well, he got whipped pretty good. I'd guess he'd stay on the move for a while. Unless there's something up here that smells like a female brown bear.

"Being up here is pretty safe. He's not as likely to check us out like he might if we were down by the river. There's nothing that should interest him other than the smell of our food, so let's wait to cook till he's had a chance to clear out. Keep your spray and rifle close, though."

While the odds are low I imagine a visit from him might be possible. In the past few hours we've not only seen bears, but we've seen them travel a long distance and their mobility makes me a bit nervous.

I watch the pair in the meadow until it's too dark to see. Witnessing what I have, has amplified my feeling that this world has a magnificent design.

We boil some water for our food pouches. I eat slowly in the light of my headlamp and turn in, settling into the bumpy surface from my sleeping bag sandwich. My pack is my pillow, my rifle rests under my arm, and the bear spray is in my hand. If a sniffing bear wakes me I'll be ready, and after this evening I can actually picture that in my mind.

The Night Speaks

I lie staring into the night sky filled with innumerable stars, minute sparkles of light. Some reflect, but most are sources of light themselves, burning on their own, creating their own brilliance. It's out there; the universe. And I am part of it, the bears and me. Small as we are, we're part of it, we belong to it.

The scene of the bears in the meadow and the fight play back in my mind over and over. It's a surreal and tangible glimpse into a world I didn't know existed and don't comprehend, like the infinite number of worlds that are out there tonight that I cannot see or even imagine. The vastness and beauty and complexity of this universe and all creation infuses me with a feeling of smallness—a grain of sand in an ocean of life. It's an overwhelming feeling of insignificance. At the same time, being a unique soul, my human spirit, infuses me with a sense of power, of worth, that is equally awe-inspiring. Feeling so small and yet so significant. My world moving amid the stars.

My life rarely reveals moments like this, emptying my mind and letting the unknown in. Even on this rock I'm moved to where I imagine a world beyond comprehension. Where I am at once feeling, and belonging to the complexity of eternity, to a destiny. I may return to bear hunting tomorrow, or maybe not.

For now, it feels simple, I'm just being.

> *I would not give a fig for the simplicity this side of complexity, but I would give my life for the simplicity on the other side of complexity.*
> —*Oliver Wendell Holmes, Jr.*

A Wild Day

With images of the bear in the meadow (and the boar that was sent packing), I wake in the predawn. I feel the cold steel of my rifle barrel next to me. It finally grows light enough to see without my headlamp and I roll out from under my tarp, dressed in my layers of clothes, ready to go.

First I scan the meadow, but it is vacant. The fight scene (as well as the love scene) from last evening is fresh in my mind. I next glass the river bottom, but the couple have moved on. Wandering is their thing in the spring.

"See anything?" Tate mumbles from under his tarp.

"Nope, looks like they've wandered off."

"Keep your eyes peeled, they might not have gone far and there's lots of cover for 'em."

I continue to glass as Tate gets up and boils some water.

"There are more out there for sure," he mumbles. "They've woken up and are wandering."

After some oatmeal Tate moves a few yards down the hill. "We need to check some of the spots we can't see from here. This is our highest point but we can't see it all."

Bear Scare

We shuffle down the gravel slope on opposite sides of a thicket of alders 50 yards below camp. Circling it is the only practical way to gain a new vantage point. Tate has moved around the west side and I've covered the east side, pausing every couple steps to glass. We both arrive at a clearing just above another alder patch. We're focused on the snow-covered slope across the river, hoping to spot a bear who's chosen this morning to move out of his den. The sun sits just above the mountain to the east and the sky is clear.

"Keep an eye on that snow slope," Tate mumbles. "You'll see nothing, nothing, and nothing, and then all of a sudden he'll be right there and you'll wonder where he came from."

This is the best viewing spot and the best weather we've had all week. The air is still and silent other than my slow breathing and the crunching of gravel under my shifting boots.

Suddenly a panicked shriek pierces the silence.

"BEAR! BEAR! BEAR!"

My binoculars drop to my chest and I follow Tate's stare down the hill. Poking up above the gray alders 30 yards below us is a huge round, brown head with two narrow, beady eyes staring at us.

A shot of adrenaline runs clear though me and I gulp a lungful of air while catching a glint of light from the sun, the exact kind of gulp and glint to produce a sneeze. And in that instant I release the biggest whole-body sneeze of my life. Tate is screaming at the bear, waving his arms and jumping up and down and yelling at me to join him.

The exhilaration of the best sneeze ever leaves me paralyzed for a moment. Then two more sneezes in quick succession. I recover my wits enough to join Tate, who is now yelling, "Don't run, don't run! Just look big and scream!" A second wave of panic hits me when I realize we're both waving empty hands—no guns or pepper spray. What the—?

The sensation of the sneezes and the panic is electrifying and I feel a momentary exhilaration I'll never forget.

The bear remains standing and staring, apparently unimpressed with our shouting, then his head disappears behind the brush.

Our arms drop and we go silent, waiting for what might happen next. "Next" comes immediately as the willowy alders between us and the bear begin shaking— he is moving directly toward us.

"RUN!" screams Tate as he pivots and sprints up the hill.

I follow, running headlong into the alder thicket we had just walked around; the most direct line back to camp. At my top terrified speed I've fallen 10 yards behind Tate. Spindly branches are slapping my face and legs. The panic of the moment has slowed time and I feel complete awareness and numbness.

Breaking out of the alder thicket I trip and stumble to my knees, slamming my hands to the rocky ground, but bounce back up, hardly missing a step. Camp is still 50 yards up the hill. My throat burns as I suck in air. In the next instant I utter the most sincere and frantic prayer of my life and everything slows down. A crystal—clear thought enters my mind—if he catches me and pulls me down, I'll roll into a ball and grab the back of My neck. If I can hold on for a few seconds Tate will be back with his gun and spray.

Instinctively I glance over my shoulder and see nothing, but don't slow down. I cover the last few yards and stumble to my gun leaning against my pack.

Tate has already chambered a round and is sweeping the hill looking for movement. Gasping for air, I chamber a round as well, but from my knees. I taste blood in my throat, like after wind sprints and just before throwing up, and my thighs burn. Then, between gasps for air, I start laughing. It's maybe a relief reflex or something, but I can't help it.

Tate is breathing hard and gives me a curious look and begins to chuckle as well. "Sorry about that. No guns, no spray, what were we thinkin'? I was sure he was comin' after us."

"No worries. Maybe he was or maybe he wasn't, but that's the most excitement I've ever had, or ever will have, and live to tell about it. But I gotta tell you, scrambling up that hill, I said the fastest prayer I've ever said. God must have something in mind for me that doesn't include getting mauled by a bear. For you too, I think."

"He's got to be close," says Tate.

With guns to our shoulders we work our way back to where we first spotted him.

My heart is still pounding in my throat, but now with a weapon my terror has turned to anticipation. Things change quickly.

There's no sign of anything on the hillside, no track, no scat, nothing. We slowly work our way around the thicket to where he first popped up and find some bent and broken undergrowth, but nothing more.

"He was here, but no telling where he went," says Tate.

We circle to the opposite side, but it seems our bear has evaporated; like a ghost.

"I'm pretty sure there was a bear, right? Like, with my sneezing I didn't make that up?"

"He was as real as I've ever seen, and closer than I've ever been without me doing the sneaking," responds Tate.

With both relief and a bit of disappointment that our bear has vanished we return to camp and resume glassing. Every nearby thicket and willows gets a good, hard look.

A couple of hours pass and the excitement that killed my appetite is gone. I'm ready to heat some water and make noodles. Usually we just graze on energy bars during the day, but since we're staying in this spot I decide to cook. We'll need a trip back to the stream for water if we stay up here tonight.

Our Bear

I'm stirring the noodles in my cup when I hear Tate whisper, "Got something. Eleven o'clock, six hundred yards out, moving right to left just below the orange brush."

I grab my binos and quickly spot the movement of tan against the rusty background, no bigger than a pencil eraser. "Looks like a bear," I whisper back, not sure why we're whispering.

"Yeah, it's a bear, but hard to tell anything else. He's not the one we just yelled at. We need a better look. Grab your gun and let's get to where he's headed.

With my gun strapped across my back to keep my hands free, we hustle down the north slope of our hill. Tate is moving fast and pauses at the bottom to find him, but a small rise blocks our line of sight.

Hunching low, we work our way through the swale up to where our bear comes into view. He's about 400 yards out and quartering toward us. Our risk of being scented is higher than that of being seen, but being seen is the one thing we control. At the moment the air is in our favor.

"If he doesn't turn he should be walking through that open draw in a few minutes. Let's get to that bunch of alders," says Tate, pointing to a spot about a hundred yards away. "That's where we need to be to get a shot."

Finding this bear and our scramble to get close has started a different kind of adrenaline rush, more controlled and calculated, more like excitement than panic. But Tate's words, "to get a shot," create a new reality for me. We're back to hunting and contemplations of the universe have vanished from my mind.

We backtrack 20 yards to a low spot and move in an arc toward the alders. Fifty yards short of the thicket we encounter a 20-foot-deep, steep, muddy ravine. We have to cross it and fast, and there is nothing faster than straight down and straight up the other side. I scoot down on my butt like on a slippery slide, slowing my speed by grabbing clumps of brush, the easy part. Climbing up the other side is tougher, scrambling in the mud and grabbing brush to pull myself up. My lungs and legs burn and the taste of blood in my throat returns.

Clearing the ravine, we stay on our knees and crawl up to the thicket to stay out of sight. We tuck in next to the alders and peek between the branches.

"There he is, straight ahead just beyond that mound in the middle." I find him through my binos while Tate pulls out his range finder. My heart is pounding. Time begins to slow down and every detail, every thought, every feeling is distinct.

"He's two hundred forty yards out. And he looks like a shooter, but that's your call. Let him get a bit closer."

The bear continues angling toward us at a steady pace over rolling mounds of straw-colored grass that's slightly lighter than his Dunn-colored fur.

I ready my rifle, frozen behind the brush, staring through my scope. My hands are shaking and my heart pounding and the crosshairs jiggle on my target. I slow everything down. Breathe, just breathe.

In a whisper I start peppering Tate with questions, "What do you think? Nice color. A shooter you say?"

"He's plenty big," Tate answers, "not a ten-footer, maybe not even nine, but he's close. He may be the best bear you'll get this close to with a rifle and a permit, and he's a good-looking bear. And we are close to the end of our time, but it's your call."

I appreciate Tate's observations and they confirm some of my own. I didn't need much convincing, just reassurance that I was seeing what he was seeing. This is one of those hunting moments of truth. I make my decision and chamber a round and steady the crosshairs on the bear. "Yeah, he's our bear. How far now?"

"One seventy. Slide around to the edge of the brush and stay low and let him get a little closer."

I scoot around to get a clear view. From a sitting position I rest my left elbow on my left knee and steady my rifle and wait. Tate picks and drops some grass to detect any breeze. There's very little and the grass falls slightly back toward him so there's no chance of being scented.

"A hundred fifty . . . hundred forty . . ." Tate whispers. "He's yours whenever you're ready, but once you shoot, keep going. Empty your gun. We can't have a wounded bear, so shoot until he's down."

I've always believed that if I took my time with the first, well-placed shot, with the right gun and ammo I wouldn't need a second, but am prepared to follow Tate's advice.

I steady my sites on the bear's left shoulder and follow as he continues to move from right to left. The crosshairs jiggle and I take a deep breath . . . then another really slow one.

"I'll try to stop him, but be ready to squeeze," whispers Tate as he covers his ears.

My thinking moves into now mode and I commit to the shot in my mind. A final exhale as Tate barks. The bear freezes and looks in our direction and I slowly squeeze. The explosion cracks the air like lightning directly overhead and the bear jumps straight in the air and spins. I know he's hit hard and I chamber another and fire, and then another. By the time the echo of the third shot fades the bear is still and on the ground.

The air is quiet again and I watch through my binos for any movement. I hear, "Good shot," from Tate. No whoops and hollers or high fives. We just sit and watch for several minutes.

"It's been a lively day," Tate continues in a low voice. "Can't remember ever having one quite like this. The unpredictability of hunting."

"Yeah, don't think I'll ever forget this. Thanks for getting us here."

"Glad we made it," Tate answers. "Yesterday at this time I was starting to wonder."

Done

Up close my bear looks bigger than from my shooting spot. From his head to his tail he is much longer than I am tall. He has thick soft fur and long claws. It's a strange feeling now that this part is over. I'm glad we found our bear, and he's a nice one, but having him on the ground signals that my adventure is mostly behind me. I'd really like to stay and soak in more of this country and the bears that live here.

Serious work always follows shooting. Taking care of the hide and meat isn't part of the fun, but it is part of the experience. Our scramble and stalk have left us about a half mile from our hilltop camp. We make our way back to retrieve our packs and gear as quickly as possible, not wanting to leave our bear to

the curiosity of any other bears who might pass by. They are out and moving so it's a real possibility.

Back on top of the knoll I survey the meadow and the rock wall, the amphitheater. I picture the bears rolling around, images I'll never forget. I've become pretty attached to this hill.

We hurry back to our bear and get to the business of skinning. Tate is doing the work and tells me to keep an eye out for more bear. With this morning's surprise encounter we're playing it safe, particularly with a bear down and the sensitive noses of others in the area. This would be easy food too, all skinned and ready to eat. Cannibalism doesn't present a moral dilemma to the bears.

Tate begins skinning and a foul odor fills the air. He explains the stench in much the same way Dok did. "These guys fatten up on salmon all summer and fall and then sleep in their dens all winter and this is what you get in the spring, stinky fish oil. But this is a dinner bell for another bear so keep your eyes peeled." I hadn't thought much about the need to stand guard, but on Tate's advice, I chamber a round of ammo and scan the horizon for any movement. We're in an open swale and have about 50 yards of visibility to the east, and about 150 yards in the other directions. Tate skins from the belly up and with half the hide removed he finds a lone bullet hole right in the kill zone.

"Looks like your first shot got him. There's no other holes so I'm guessing your other two missed."

"The first shot felt solid. And with him jumping and spinning I'm not surprised the others missed."

Visitor

I keep watch in a clockwise pattern over and over. On my third rotation I freeze. Up a small rise to the east only 40 yards away a huge round head rises above the grass, like a harvest moon coming up on the horizon. Stretching to his full height on two legs is the biggest bear I have ever seen, dead or alive. He seems tentative, like he's trying to sneak a peek at us and not be seen. Given his size, concealment is not possible anywhere other than in the thickets by the river.

"Got company, Tate," I whisper, pulling my rifle to my shoulder. Tate looks up and drops his skinning knife, grabs his rifle and jumps to his feet. At this motion the bear drops and disappears and Tate starts running toward where it was standing. "We gotta see where he goes," he shouts.

I follow, stumbling across the uneven spongy turf as fast as I can. We cover the distance in about fifteen seconds, just in time to see the bear's butt bouncing down the hill toward the river. He's 200 yards away and the irony that we are now chasing the bear is not lost on me.

"Could this get any crazier?" I laugh, hunched over trying to catch my breath. "A couple hours ago we're running from one bear, then we stalk another bear, and now we're chasing a third. That's crazy."

"Won't disagree with that," Tate chuckles back. "Guess he smelled our bear and came to check us out. Running off like that is what they usually do. We've had a good day with bears—a week of nothing other than a few tracks and now they're all over."

We return to our bear and Tate gets back to work.

A couple of long, sweaty hours later we roll the hide into a ball and tie it to the top of Tate's pack. The head and skull stay intact until we can get back to camp and take our time with the more delicate work. But the skinning Tate has done here in the field was fast and skillful.

"We gotta get to a high spot and see if we can radio Bill. If we can connect we'll arrange a pickup, hopefully this afternoon." We find a small rise and Tate breaks out the radio. Bill's indistinguishable voice crackles on the other end and I hear Tate's side of the conversation, describing our location.

"Yeah we had some luck. It's a good story. We're just north of the westernmost mountain, close to the river. We'll be the two guys who look dead worn out."

Bill is familiar with every acre of this country and knows where he'll find us. He instructs Tate to find a spot for him to land. With no obvious flat and open space in view we head west with our guns loaded and on guard.

Tate stops by a trickle of water and surveys a meadow, "This should work."

"Looks pretty lumpy to me."

"Bill won't have any problem with it. He can land on most anything."

We drop our packs and sit to wait.

"This spot looks familiar," I say in a tired voice.

"Yeah, we came through here about this time yesterday. About two hundred yards to the south is where we filled up with water. Been a pretty awesome day. Seems like longer ago, doesn't it?"

"Yes it does."

The sky has become overcast again. The air is mild and I close my eyes and feel myself sink into the soft tundra under me. I don't want to leave, but know I'll soon hear the hum of Bill's plane. And then comes the business of packing up and flying out. The quiet will fade. The feelings and the memory, and the story will be all that remains.

As a newcomer to the world of bear hunting, and without any particular draw to it, I've been caught up in the fascination of being out where it's this wild. Where life is unpredictable. Where there's little or no plan— just wandering, watching, and soaking it in. This is a freedom I want to keep, even if just in my mind. Then comes the hum of the plane, and the feeling evaporates.

Tate waves and Bill circles and drops to 50 feet coming in from the south, and slows to a hover over the grass flats, bounces, rolls to a stop, and spins around. The door pops open and he climbs down to the grass, waiting for us to approach with our gear. Tate gets to the plane first and before I can join them I see Bill looking in my direction and grinning.

"So, Tate tells me you almost shook hands with a bear."

"I thought you said to stay quiet about that."

"Well, thought I better come clean," says Tate.

"Yeah, that will go down as one of the highlights of my life, and you can trust the story will get bigger and the escape narrower the more I tell it."

"Well, it wouldn't be a story if it didn't," Bill laughs. "Let's get loaded and back to camp. Mick is missing you two."

Bill loads my gear and the bear and I slide into the cramped rear seat. Tate moves back a few steps and Bill cranks the engine. We bounce across the grass, catch some air, and circle back to the north and rise to 500 feet.

"So, you had a good hunt?" Bill shouts over the radio.

"The best, no way it could've been any better." And I feel a shiver down my spine and smile. It really couldn't have been better.

The flight back seems quick and as we float down to the landing strip I see Mick on the front deck. We unload and Bill heads back for Tate. I spread the hide on the ground to dry.

"Looks like you got a nice one," Mick says.

"Yup, pretty bear," I respond, not wanting to say much more. I grab the sack of salt from the shed and flip the hide over, flesh side up, and spread the salt. There'll be plenty of work fleshing out the skull when Tate returns so my only goal right now is to get it cool and drying and the salt is my best tool.

The items I unloaded are in the shed where I left them. I rummage through it for some soap and a hand towel to get some of the blood and dirt washed off.

Within an hour comes the hum of the plane. Things are busy for the next couple of hours, capping the head and getting more salt into the crevices, and reorganizing gear.

"You good to head out in the morning?" Bill asks. "I got some hunters coming in around noon. I can fly you out when I pick them up and you can get on your way, or you're welcome to stay if you want more of Mick's cooking."

"I'm good to go whenever you do. I should get back to the kids."

My legs are beat and I plunk down in a camp chair and watch Tate skin the head and turn the face inside out and give it a good salting. It's much more surgical than I'd imagined.

"You done many of those?" I ask.

"Yeah, a few. We should let him sit out until dark and then wrap him up so varmints don't chew on him in the night. Then we'll resalt him in the morning for the trip out."

Mick's meal is a repeat version of his stew from last week, but compared to our cooking on the tundra is a little tastier.

I move back up to my tent and sit and listen to the quiet. It's so quiet. This past day has been one I'll never forget. Sleep tonight will be easy.

****

It's early on my final morning and the sleep on the cot was heaven. You come to appreciate those little things. I wake to the same predawn sky from a week ago, but feel like a different person. The scene is nearly identical with my star in the middle. I've lived the metaphor this past week and now feel elevated in a way. Fully alive. I get to work gathering my gear and the final salting of the hide and skull for transport. Tate approaches with a cup of coffee, the steam rising with an aroma that complements the morning air.

"Looks like you're about ready. That salt should keep the hair good and tight but you might want to get it in your freezer when you get back, at least until you send it to be tanned. What are your plans for the skull?"

"Not sure. Guess I'll get it cleaned up and just set it on a shelf. Haven't thought of that yet."

"I have a buddy in Anchorage who has beetles that'll clean it up real good if you want. He charges a hundred bucks plus whatever it costs to mail it to you when it's ready."

"Works for me. I'll just leave it with you?"

"Yup."

I reach in my pocket and retrieve a small roll of bills and a new knife, and hand it to Tate. "This is for you. There's a little extra thanks there in appreciation for the close encounter and adrenaline rush. I won't soon forget that."

Tate gives me an, "Are you serious?" squint and sees that I am and thanks me. I pause for a minute, "Also, thanks for the education on the bears, and for sharing some of your beliefs. I appreciate hearing them."

He smiles and nods without any words. I grab my pack and gun and head toward the plane and Tate follows with the bag containing the salted hide.

Bill loads the gear and I climb up to the rear seat. He shouts over his shoulder that he'll be back in a couple of hours. Mick and Tate give a wave as we take off.

****

The flight back to the airstrip seems much shorter than the trip out. We arrive to find Dok unloading and loading as he had a week ago and talking to the fresh ears milling around their gear.

Bill introduces me to his clients, a small woman and her husband, with a bow case and a rifle.

"So you found one," remarks the man nodding to my lumpy bag with the hide.

"Yeah, all our action was in the last two days and then we saw six. They're definitely out now. You should see plenty. So you're going after them with a bow?"

"Well, my wife is. I'll just back her up with the rifle. She's taken three with her bow so far," he adds casually. They don't look like folks inclined to tall tales.

A few more minutes of small talk and I learn that he's a dentist, and has hunted bear many times, a few of them with Tate. I connect the dots and realize this is the dentist that's the source of Tate's expanded knowledge of bears.

"I learned quite a bit about bears out there this past week from Tate. And he said a lot of that came from you."

"Yeah, Tate and I have spent quite a few hours glassing and I can't keep from talking about bears."

"Well, you taught Tate well." For an instant I think of the anticipation of heading out with a bow, but quickly dismiss the idea.

Rick is over by his plane waiting for me. I thank Bill and shake hands. "Let me know when you're ready for your next bear," Bill smiles.

"Will do," I say, knowing my past week really has been my once-in-a-lifetime. I loved it and what I found out there on the tundra, but there will be no more bears for me. And I could never have another experience like this in a million years, so I won't try. I'll stumble on to other adventures. I have no clue at this point what they might be, but they're out there. They seem to just come along when I keep my eyes open and ask, "Why not?"

I head over to Rick's plane and load up. Within a few minutes we are in the air headed back to Anchorage. My mind wanders back to my last thought. Once in a lifetime. I've had a few and expect to have more before I'm done, and I'm OK with that.

There's a design to life, and mine in particular, that's hard to understand in the moment. It won't likely make much sense until it's farther in the rearview mirror. I can't quickly recall the best highlight of this hunt. It all felt so rich. Maybe the bears in the meadow by the rock wall. Being able to watch their wild world and the wonder of their existence. That's probably it. Knowing they are out there; magnificent animals that they are. It's easy to see why they are revered by the Natives and have earned their highest respect. They have mine as well.

As long as I watch for the rose colored glow of a new day on the horizon, adventures will appear in my path.

Keep close to Nature's heart… and break clear away, once in a while, and climb a mountain or spend a week in the woods. Wash your spirit clean.
John Muir

Alaska Brown Bear